Secure The Bag
7 Keys To Financial Freedom
&
Investing Wisely For A Successful Life.

By
Richmond Sterling

Copyright © 2023 Richmond Sterling

Acknowledgments

I am deeply grateful for the incredible support and encouragement I received while writing "Secure The Bag: 7 Keys To Financial Freedom and Investing Wisely For A Successful Life." This book would not have been possible without the support of some individuals.

First and foremost, I want to thank God the giver of wisdom, and my family for their unwavering support and understanding during this journey of making this book a reality.

I extend my heartfelt appreciation to the financial experts and mentors whose wisdom and guidance shaped the content of this book. Your insights have been invaluable.

To my friends and colleagues who provided feedback and encouragement, thank you for your invaluable input.

Finally, I want to acknowledge the readers and supporters who believe in the message of financial empowerment and success. Your enthusiasm motivates me to continue spreading the message of financial freedom.

Thank you to all who played a part in making this book a reality. Your support is deeply appreciated.

~ **Richmond Sterling**

Introduction

"Secure The Bag: *7 Keys To Financial Freedom and Investing Wisely For A Successful Life*" by Richmond Sterling is a comprehensive guide that unlocks the secrets to financial success. In this book, you'll embark on a journey to build a solid financial foundation, make wise financial decisions and investments, and achieve the keys to financial freedom. With a focus on income generation, debt management, and philanthropy, you'll learn how to secure your financial future while also gaining insights into strategies for living a successful life. Whether you're just starting your financial journey or looking to enhance your wealth-building skills, this book offers a roadmap to help you reach your financial goals.

"Secure The Bag" by Richmond Sterling is a comprehensive guide, encompassing five distinct parts with multiple chapters in each, covering a wide range of topics on financial freedom and wise investing for a successful life. This book provides a holistic approach to mastering your finances and securing your future.

Foreword

In the ever-evolving landscape of personal finance and investment, Richmond Sterling's "*Secure The Bag*" serves as a beacon of guidance and wisdom. In this comprehensive journey through the realms of financial freedom and wise investing, Sterling provides readers with the keys to unlocking a successful life. With an unwavering commitment to empowering individuals, this book traverses the essential terrain of building a strong financial foundation, making sound investments, and achieving genuine financial freedom.

Sterling's meticulous breakdown of the seven keys to financial freedom ensures that no stone is left unturned. From mastering income generation to understanding the intricacies of tax planning, this book is a roadmap to financial prosperity. Beyond wealth accumulation, Sterling delves into the art of giving back and fostering a spirit of philanthropy, reinforcing the notion that financial success is intertwined with contributing positively to the world.

The journey doesn't stop at financial prowess. Sterling goes further, addressing the holistic aspects of life and success, from mindset and time management to building meaningful relationships and striking that elusive work-life balance.

"Secure The Bag" doesn't just lay out a plan; it guides you through the process of creating your financial freedom plan and sustaining it for the long term. This book is more than a financial manual; it's a life-changing tool that equips you to navigate the complex world of personal finance, offering a brighter future and a secure bag for all who embark on this transformative journey.

Richmond Sterling's wisdom, knowledge, and passion for financial freedom resonate throughout these pages. Whether you're just starting your journey or looking to enhance your financial wisdom, "Secure The Bag" is your trusted companion. Prepare to embark on a life-changing expedition. Let's secure the bag together.

~ Richmond Sterling

Table of Contents

Introduction 7
Foreword...7
Why Financial Freedom Matters 7
Part I: Building a Strong Financial Foundation............7
Chapter 1: Setting Financial Goals..............................7
Chapter 2: Budgeting and Financial Planning.............7
Chapter 3: Emergency Funds and Savings...................7
Part II: Investing Wisely...7
Chapter 4: Understanding Investment Basics..............7
Chapter 5: Types of Investments.................................7
Chapter 6: Risk Management in Investing....................7
Part III: Keys to Financial Freedom............................7
Chapter 7: Key 1 - Income Generation........................7
Chapter 8: Key 2 - Debt Management..........................7
Chapter 9: Key 3 - Building Multiple Income Streams...7
Chapter 10: Key 4 - Asset Accumulation.....................7
Chapter 11: Key 5 - Tax Planning................................7
Chapter 12: Key 6 - Retirement Planning 7
Chapter 13: Key 7 - Giving Back and Philanthropy.......7
Part IV: Strategies for a Successful Life 7
Chapter 14: Mindset and Success................................7
Chapter 15: Time Management 7
Chapter 16: Networking and Building Relationships.....7

Chapter 17: Balancing Work and Life..7
Part V: Putting It All Together 7
Chapter 18: Creating Your Financial Freedom Plan 7
Chapter 19: Sustaining Financial Freedom 7
Conclusion..7
Recommendation..7
Review Enquiry..7
Acknowledgments 1

Table of Contents

Acknowledgments
.... 2
Introduction
....
4

Foreword
....
. 6
Why Financial Freedom
Matters 14
Part I: Building a Strong
Financial
Foundation.......................
.... 15
Chapter 1: Setting Financial
Goals 15
Chapter 2: Budgeting and
Financial
Planning...........................
.... 20
Chapter 3: Emergency Funds and
Savings.............................
.... 24
Part II: Investing Wisely
.... 29
Chapter 4: Understanding
Investment
Basics.............................
.... 29
Chapter 5: Types of
Investments............... 37
Chapter 6: Risk Management in
Investing...........................
.... 39
Part III: Keys to Financial
Freedom 42
Chapter 7: Key 1 - Income
Generation 42

Chapter 8: Key 2 - Debt Management 46

Chapter 9: Key 3 - Building Multiple Income Streams 50

Chapter 10: Key 4 - Asset Accumulation 55

Chapter 11: Key 5 - Tax Planning 59

Chapter 12: Key 6 - Retirement Planning 63

Chapter 13: Key 7 - Giving Back and Philanthropy 69

Part IV: Strategies for a Successful Life ... 73

Chapter 14: Mindset and Success 73

Chapter 15: Time Management 77

Chapter 16: Networking and Building Relationships 81

Chapter 17: Balancing Work and Life 86

Part V: Putting It All Together 90

Chapter 18: Creating Your Financial Freedom Plan

....
.... 90
Chapter 19: Sustaining Financial Freedom ... 94
Conclusion
....
99
Recommendation ....
.... 100
Review Enquiry
.... 101

Why Financial Freedom Matters

Financial freedom matters because it provides individuals with the ability to make choices without being constrained by financial limitations. It offers peace of mind, the opportunity to pursue one's goals, and the ability to weather unexpected financial challenges.

~ **Richmond Sterling**

Part I: Building a Strong Financial Foundation

Chapter 1: Setting Financial Goals

Setting financial objectives is a critical step toward financial security and well-being. In this chapter, we will look at the necessity of having clear and attainable financial objectives, as well as how they relate to achieving financial freedom and living a successful life.

1. **Financial Freedom**: Financial freedom is defined as having enough financial resources and stability to make choices and live the life you want without being bound by financial constraints. It entails being able to pay your bills, save for the future, and pursue your passions and ambitions without financial concern.

2. **The Importance of Financial Goal Setting**

- Clarity and Direction: Setting financial objectives gives you a clear sense of direction. It assists you in determining your financial goals for the short and long term.

- Motivation: Goals are used to motivate people. When you have a particular financial goal in mind, it is easier to stay disciplined and work towards it.

- Measuring success: Setting financial goals allows you to track your success. You can monitor your progress toward your goals and alter your financial plans as needed.

- Prioritization: Goal-setting assists you in prioritizing what is most essential to you. This could involve things like purchasing a home, supporting your children's education, or retiring comfortably.

3. Different types of financial goals

- Short-Term Goals: These normally have a one-year or less time frame and may include developing an emergency fund or paying off credit card debt.

- Medium-Term Goals: These objectives typically last one to five years and can include saving for a down payment on a house or planning a large vacation.

- Long-Term Goals: Long-term goals span five years or more and frequently include retirement planning, major asset accumulation, and leaving a financial legacy for your family.

4. Setting SMART Goals

- Specific: Goals should be defined and specific. Let's say I want to save $15,000. The $15,000 becomes the goal.

- Measurable: Your given goals should be measurable with your available resources at the moment so that you can track your progress from time to time. For example, "I will save $800 each month" is quantifiable to the given goal of $15,000.

- Achievable: Based on your existing financial condition, your goals should be practical and reachable.

- Related: Your goals should be related to your life and dreams. They should be consistent with your values.

- Time-Bound: Establish a timeframe for attaining your objectives.

5. Financial Planning Tools:
Further chapters will expose you to numerous financial planning

tools and approaches to help you achieve your goals, such as budgeting, investing, and debt management.

6. **Financial Freedom and Success**: Attaining financial objectives is are critical step toward financial freedom. Financial independence entails having enough money to live life on your own terms, whether it means following a dream career, touring the world, or retiring early.

Finally, Chapter 1 on Setting Financial Goals lays the groundwork for financial success and freedom. By comprehending the value of creating clear objectives, adhering to the SMART criteria, and matching your financial aspirations with your life's vision, you lay the framework for a prosperous life filled with financial security and freedom.

Chapter 2: Budgeting and Financial Planning

Budgeting and financial planning are critical components of gaining financial freedom and living a prosperous life. In this chapter, we'll look at how budgeting and financial planning can help you manage your money, build wealth, and eventually achieve financial freedom.

1. **Financial Freedom Defined**: Financial freedom is the ability to make decisions in life without being constrained by financial limitations. It means having control over your money rather than being controlled by your money.

2. **Budgeting**

- Definition: Budgeting is the process of constructing an income and expense plan. It assists you in allocating your money and prioritizing your financial goals.

   - Importance: Budgeting allows you to keep track of your spending, eliminate unnecessary expenses, and make sure you're saving and investing for the future.

3. **Financial Planning**

- Definition: Financial planning is a broad term that includes budgeting. Setting financial goals, developing a plan to accomplish those goals, and making decisions regarding investments, insurance, and retirement planning are all part of the process.

- Importance: Effective financial planning assists you in allocating your money resources to your life objectives. It guarantees that you arc well-prepared for crises and that you save and invest appropriately.

4. **Budgeting and Financial Planning Procedures**

- Establish Specific Goals: Establish short-term and long-term financial objectives. These may include purchasing a home, investing for retirement, or launching a business.

- Develop a Budget: Create a detailed budget including your income, spending, and savings. This will allow you to see where your money is going and where you can cut back.

- Emergency Fund: Create a fund to meet unforeseen expenses. This keeps you from going into debt in the event of an emergency.

- Invest Wisely: Set aside a percentage of your earnings for assets like stocks, bonds, or real estate. This allows your funds to expand over time.

- Risk Management: Consider your insurance alternatives to safeguard your possessions and loved ones.

- Retirement Planning: Start saving for retirement as soon as possible to ensure a pleasant life after work.

- Periodic Review: Review your budget and financial plan regularly to make required adjustments depending on changing circumstances.

5. The Advantages of Budgeting and Financial Planning

- Financial Security: You are better prepared for financial emergencies if you manage your money effectively.

- Debt Reduction: Budgeting allows you to pay off bills more quickly.
- Wealth Creation: With proper financial planning, you can increase your wealth through investments.
- Financial Peace of Mind: Knowing you have a good financial plan in place helps alleviate financial stress.

In conclusion, Chapter 2 underlines the need for budgeting and financial planning in obtaining financial independence. You may take control of your finances and work toward a successful life where you have the flexibility to pursue your aspirations and ambitions without being hampered by financial restraints by defining clear goals, developing a budget, and making informed financial decisions.

Chapter 3: Emergency Funds and Savings

Savings and emergency funds are essential components of

obtaining financial freedom and success in life. In this chapter, we'll look at the significance of emergency money and savings, how they contribute to financial security, and how they play a part in long-term financial success.

1. **Emergency Funds**: An emergency fund is a separate savings account set up to handle unforeseen expenses or crises like medical bills, car repairs, or job loss. It serves as a financial safety net, keeping you from falling into debt when life throws you unexpected curve balls. Having an emergency fund is essential because it gives you peace of mind and prevents you from having to rely on high-interest credit cards or loans during an emergency.

   - The Role of Emergency Funds in Financial Freedom: Emergency funds promote financial stability while also reducing stress. When you have a safety net in place, you can make sensible financial decisions without worrying about going into debt. This allows you to maintain control over your financial life, which is a vital component of financial freedom.

2. **Regular Savings**: Saving money regularly is a basic practice for financial success. This chapter emphasizes the significance of consistently saving aside a portion of your income. Saving money, whether through automated transfers to a savings account or other techniques, ensures that you create wealth over time.

- The Role of Regular Savings for Financial Freedom: Regular Savings are the foundation of financial independence. They let you work toward financial objectives including purchasing a home, starting a business, or retiring comfortably. Without funds, reaching these objectives becomes difficult, if not impossible.

3. **Compound Interest**: The chapter may also go into the benefits of compound interest. Because of the compounding effect, money saved and carefully invested can grow over time. This means that you are not only saving for the future but

also laying the groundwork for future financial success.

- Compound Interest's Role in Financial Freedom: Understanding and capitalizing on compound interest is critical for long-term financial success. When you invest intelligently, your money may work for you and your wealth can expand dramatically. This is an important step toward financial independence because your investments create passive income.

4. **Budgeting and Prioritization**: It is critical to emphasize the relationship between budgeting and savings in this chapter. A well-structured budget assists you in allocating funds to savings, ensuring that your financial cushion is constantly built.

- The Role of Budgeting in Financial Freedom: Budgeting allows you to control your expenses, minimize wasteful spending, and direct money toward savings and investments. It is an essential instrument for gaining financial freedom since it assures that you have control over your financial decisions.

5. **Long-Term Goals**: The chapter should emphasize the need to establish long-term financial goals. Having a clear picture of what you're saving for inspires you to be disciplined in your savings and investment plans, whether it's retirement planning, buying a home, or investing in your children's education.

- The Role in Financial Freedom: Long-term goals give your financial path meaning. They provide you the motivation to save, invest, and make short-term sacrifices for the sake of long-term financial freedom.

In conclusion, Chapter 3: Emergency Funds and Savings is a critical guide to financial success and financial freedom. It emphasizes the significance of saving regularly, understanding the power of compound interest, budgeting efficiently, and developing long-term financial objectives. These behaviors not only assure financial security, but also pave the route for a happy and full life.

Part II: Investing Wisely

Chapter 4: Understanding Investment Basics

Understanding Investment Basics is likely to concentrate on essential topics connected to financial independence and prudent investing.

1. **Financial Freedom**: In the context of investing wisely for a successful life, financial freedom implies being able to maintain your desired lifestyle and meet your financial goals without being bound by money. It entails making smart investment decisions that develop your wealth over time, providing a solid income and security, and ultimately allowing you to live the life you want without continual financial concerns. Saving and investing for retirement, creating passive income streams, and managing your investments intelligently can all contribute to long-term financial success.

2. **Investment ideas**: It will almost certainly include core investment ideas such as diversification, risk management, and the power of compounding, all of which are critical for wealth creation.

i. Diversification: To mitigate risk, diversify your investments across multiple assets or asset types. It mitigates the impact of a single investment's bad performance on your portfolio.

ii. Risk Management: Risk management is critical in investing. It entails identifying and reducing potential risks linked with investments to maintain capital and meet long-term financial objectives.

iii. The Power of Compounding: Compounding refers to your investment's ability to generate earnings and then reinvest those earnings to generate additional earnings. Compounding can dramatically increase the growth of your money over time, making it an important principle for long-term investors.

3. **Asset Classes**: This category comprises several asset classes such as stocks, bonds, and real

estate, as well as their responsibilities in a well-rounded investment portfolio.

Here's a quick rundown of these asset groups and their respective functions in a well-rounded investment portfolio:

i. Stocks: - Stocks indicate ownership in a firm.

- They have the potential for significant profits but are more risky owing to market changes.

- Stocks are vital for long-term growth and can assist in the accumulation of wealth over time.

Bonds are debt securities in which investors lend money to governments or corporations in exchange for monthly interest payments and the repayment of the principal at maturity.

- Bonds are often regarded as less risky than stocks, and they give income and stability to a portfolio. They help to preserve capital and generate income.

iii. Real Estate: Buying residential, commercial, or industrial real estate is a type of real estate investment.

- Real estate can provide rental income as well as prospective property value appreciation.

- It diversifies a portfolio and protects against inflation.

To accomplish diversity and risk management, a well-rounded investment portfolio incorporates a combination of different asset groups. Stocks provide potential for growth, bonds provide stability, and real estate can increase income while protecting against inflation. Balancing these assets can assist you in making good investments for long-term financial success.

4. **Long-Term Perspective**: Maintaining investments over a longer period, frequently years or decades, with the awareness that short-term market swings are common and may be overcome over time. This strategy emphasizes patience, diversity, and the power of compounding to consistently grow wealth and weather market ups and downs.

5. **Investment techniques**: Although investment techniques vary greatly, two prominent ways are passive index investing and active stock picking.

Pros of Investing in Passive Indexes:

i. Diversification: By investing in a broad market index, it distributes risk.

ii. Low costs and Expenses: Typically has fewer costs and expenses.

iii. Stable Returns: Aims to match the performance of the market.

Cons:

i. Limited Control: There is a limited opportunity to outperform the market.

ii. No Individual Selection: It is not possible to target certain stocks or assets.

Pros of Active Stock Selection:

i. High Return Potential: Skilled managers can outperform the market.

ii. Customization: Allows for the selection of individual stocks.

Cons:

i. Increased costs: Management fees can be substantial.

ii. Underperformance Risk: Many active managers fail to outperform the market.

iii. Time-consuming: Constant research and monitoring are required.

Individual goals, risk tolerance, and time commitment all play a role in determining the best plan. Diversifying between both passive and active techniques can be a wise investment strategy.

Setting financial objectives is an important component of investing intelligently for a successful life. Here's a quick rundown:

1. Define Your Financial Objectives: Begin by establishing your financial objectives, such as purchasing a home, retiring comfortably, or supporting your children's school.

2. Classify Goals: Differentiate between short-term (1-3 years), medium-term (3-5 years), and long-term (5+ years) objectives.

3. Quantify Goals: Assign monetary values and dates to your objectives. As a result, they are more actionable.

4. Risk Tolerance: Determine your level of risk tolerance. Long-term goals may need riskier investments, whilst short-term aims should be more conservative.

5. Diversification: To manage risk, diversify your investing

portfolio. Different assets, such as stocks, bonds, and real estate, should be aligned with your objectives.

6. Regular Review: Monitor and alter your assets regularly to ensure they are in line with your changing financial goals and risk tolerance.

You may boost your chances of long-term financial success by matching your investing decisions with your financial goals and risk tolerance.

7. Risk Tolerance: Risk tolerance refers to a person's aptitude and willingness to tolerate changes in the value of their investments. It is an important aspect of making sensible investing decisions for a prosperous financial life. Understanding your risk tolerance allows you to select assets that correspond to your level of comfort, ensuring that you can stay involved for the long term without making rash decisions during market volatility. To reach your financial objectives, you must establish a balance between risk and potential rewards.

Chapter 5: Types of Investments

This section discusses the many investment alternatives available to individuals. It usually discusses:

1. **Stocks**: Stocks indicate ownership in a firm and can provide large returns.

2. **Bonds**: Debt instruments in which you lend money to a company or government in exchange for periodic interest payments.

3. **Real Estate**: Purchasing tangible properties such as houses, apartments, or commercial real estate.

4. **Mutual Funds**: A pooled investment vehicle that pools funds from different individuals to invest in a diverse portfolio of stocks, bonds, or other securities.

5. **Exchange-exchanged Funds (ETFs)**: These are similar to mutual funds, except they are exchanged on stock exchanges like individual equities.

Commodities are investments in tangible items such as gold, oil, or agricultural products.

7. **Options and derivatives**: Complicated financial instruments whose value is derived from an underlying asset.

8. **Cryptocurrencies**: Digital currencies with volatile prices, such as Bitcoin and Ethereum.

Chapter 6: Risk Management in Investing

Investing risk management entails strategies and procedures for minimizing the potential negative impact of investments. Here are some major concepts that are frequently discussed in risk management.

1. **Risk Assessment**: Recognizing and evaluating the many types of risks associated with investing, such as market risk, credit risk, and liquidity risk.

2. **Diversification**: To limit risk, it is important to distribute investments across several asset classes (stocks, bonds, and real

estate). The chapter might go over the advantages of not placing all of your eggs in one basket.

3. **Risk Tolerance**: Assessing your risk tolerance and aligning your investment strategy with your level of risk tolerance. This will differ from person to person.

4. **Asset Allocation**: Going over the notion of allocating assets depending on your investing objectives, time horizon, and risk tolerance.

5. **Risk Mitigation Strategies**: Investigating techniques like stop-loss orders, hedging, and the use of defensive stocks to limit possible losses.

6. **Long-term Perspective**: Stressing the significance of a long-term investment horizon and how it might assist in alleviating short-term market swings.

7. **Insurance and Emergency Funds**: Discuss how insurance and an emergency fund can be used as part of a larger risk management strategy to defend against unexpected financial shocks.

8. **Behavioral Finance**: This course covers the psychological components of risk management, such as how emotions can influence financial decisions.

9. **Monitoring and Adjustment**: Explaining the need to review and adjust your investment portfolio regularly to ensure it is aligned with your goals and risk tolerance.

Part III: Keys to Financial Freedom

Chapter 7: Key 1 - Income Generation

Income Generation as a Key to Financial Freedom for a Successful Life.

In this chapter, we will look at the critical role that income creation plays in obtaining financial independence and living a successful life. Income production is a critical component of personal finance and wealth management because it provides the major source of financial resources for fulfilling one's objectives and desires. Let us explain why revenue generation is such an important aspect of financial success:

1. **Financial Security**: Earning an income provides a safety net, ensuring that you can cover your essential expenses and have a financial cushion in case of an emergency. This security serves as the cornerstone for your financial freedom.

2. **Wealth Accumulation**: A consistent income enables you to save and invest, both of which are necessary for wealth accumulation. Investing your income effectively can lead to asset growth and, over time, wealth generation.

3. **Debt Management**: Having a steady revenue stream allows you to manage and pay off debts, which is essential for reaching financial independence. Debts can be a huge burden, and earning an income is the only way to get rid of them.

4. **Opportunity Creation**: Having a source of income allows you to take advantage of possibilities, such as starting a

business, investing in education, or making other investments that will help you achieve your financial goals.

5. **Financial Independence**: Earning money is a step toward financial independence. It enables you to rely on your own resources rather than those of others, which is a key component of financial independence.

6. **Life Quality**: Your money has a direct impact on your life quality. It allows you to enjoy adventures, buy things and services, and support your family, all of which contribute to a happy and satisfying existence.

7. **Retirement Planning**: Income generating is critical for retirement planning. You can develop a retirement fund that provides a pleasant and stress-free retirement by consistently saving and investing a portion of your salary.

8. **Long-Term Goals**: Income creation is required to achieve long-term financial goals such as purchasing a home, sending your children to college, or traveling around the world. Your income

is the motor that propels you toward your goals.

9. **Flexibility and Choices**: Having a steady income gives you more options and flexibility in your life. It allows you to explore your passions, take reasonable risks, and make decisions that are consistent with your principles.

10. **Peace of Mind**: Knowing that you have a steady stream of income can alleviate financial stress and bring peace of mind. This mental and emotional well-being is an important part of living a successful life.

Finally, Chapter 7 emphasizes the importance of revenue generating as a pillar of financial freedom and success. It emphasizes how income generation enables individuals to protect their financial security, pursue their desires, and live a life that is consistent with their goals and values. Understanding the significance of money production and managing it intelligently is a critical step toward financial independence and overall life success.

Chapter 8: Key 2 - Debt Management

Debt Management as a Key to Financial Freedom for a Successful Life

Debt management is an essential part of gaining financial independence and living a successful life. In this chapter, we'll look at the importance of debt management and how it can help you achieve financial success.

1. **Debt Definition**: Debt is money borrowed with the commitment to repay it, usually with interest. It can take the shape of credit card debt, school loans, mortgages, or personal loans. When utilized appropriately, debt can be a valuable financial tool, such as for investments in school or property. However, if not properly managed, it can rapidly become a burden.

2. **Debt as a Dual-Edged Sword**: Debt can help you attain significant life goals like purchasing a home, starting a

business, or furthering your education. Excessive and poorly managed debt, on the other hand, can stymie your financial growth. It can result in large interest payments, stress, and limited financial flexibility.

3. **Debt Management Strategies**: To use debt as a stepping stone to financial freedom, you must employ the following strategies:

-   Budgeting: Make a reasonable budget to guarantee that you can satisfy your debt commitments while also covering other expenses.

-   Pay Off High-Interest Debt First: To lessen your financial load, prioritize paying off high-interest bills first.

-   Avoiding needless Debt: Avoid incurring needless debt, such as overspending on credit cards.

-   Emergency Fund: Create an emergency fund to cover unforeseen expenses without incurring further debt.

4. **Good Debt vs. Bad Debt**: Not all debt is the same. Good debt often consists of long-term investments, such as a mortgage

or company loan. High-interest consumer debt is an example of bad debt because it drains your cash without adding value.

5. **Financial Freedom and Debt Reduction**: Reducing and eventually eliminating debt is an important step toward financial freedom. When you are debt-free, you have more money to save, invest, and enjoy life without continual financial concerns.

6. **Wealth Creation**: Once you've handled your debt, you may redirect your efforts to wealth creation. This could include investments, savings, and passive income options. Debt management is the cornerstone for creating a more secure financial future.

7. **Achieving Goals**: Debt management enables you to achieve your financial and personal objectives. Controlling your finances is critical to success, whether you want to retire comfortably, travel the world, or pursue your passions.

Finally, Chapter 8 underscores the significance of proper debt management in obtaining financial freedom and living a prosperous life. You can pave the road for a more secure and prosperous future by recognizing the difference between good and bad debt, applying sensible financial plans, and working toward debt reduction. Debt management is not only a financial duty, but also a necessary step in realizing your objectives and aspirations.

Chapter 9: Key 3 - Building Multiple Income Streams

Building Multiple Income Streams as a Key to Financial Freedom for a Successful Life

In this chapter, we'll look at the notion of creating several revenue streams and why it's so important for obtaining financial freedom and success in life. The term "multiple income streams" refers to having other sources of income in addition to your principal employment or business. These additional income streams might come from investments, side hustles, passive income, and other sources. Let us expand on the significance of this method for financial success:

1. **Risk Mitigation and Diversification**: Relying entirely on one source of income is dangerous. If that source is compromised or lost, it can result in financial difficulties. Creating several income streams helps to diversify your cash sources, lowering your reliance on a single organization or profession.

2. **Income Stability**: Having multiple sources of income provides a more robust financial basis. Even if one stream suffers a decline, others may compensate. This consistency can help to alleviate financial stress and worry.

3. **Accelerated Wealth Creation**: Having various revenue streams helps hasten the growth of wealth. The extra income can be put toward investments, savings, and debt reduction, allowing you to accumulate wealth more quickly.

4. **Financial Security**: Financial freedom and prosperity are frequently the result of security. You are better prepared to deal

with unforeseen bills, medical emergencies, or job loss if you have various income streams. This sense of security contributes to a general sense of accomplishment and well-being.

5. **Expanded Financial Chances**: With more money, you can pursue additional chances for personal and professional development. You can invest in education, create your own business, or pursue ventures that interest you, increasing your prospects of success in different aspects of life.

6. **Reduced Financial Stress**: Financial stress can be a major impediment to success. Multiple income streams can reduce stress by ensuring you have enough resources to meet your requirements and goals, enabling you to focus on personal and professional development.

7. **Passive Income**: Creating passive income streams, such as rental income from real estate or dividends from investments, is an important element of diversifying your income. Passive income needs less engagement on a daily

basis, leaving you more time for other pastimes and interests.

8. **Long-Term Sustainability**: Having multiple revenue streams can help you be financially stable in the long run. You'll be better able to adjust to changing economic conditions and market changes if you diversify your revenue sources.

9. **Personal Development**: Pursuing numerous income streams frequently entails learning new skills, managing assets, and taking measured risks. Personal and professional development is an essential component of achieving life success.

10. **Lifestyle Options**: Having several income streams allows you to make lifestyle decisions that reflect your values and wants. You have the option of working less, spending more time with family, traveling, or participating in activities that add to your happiness and overall well-being.

Finally, Chapter 9 underscores the importance of creating various revenue streams in order to achieve financial freedom and success in life. It not only provides financial security, but it also opens up prospects for personal growth and fulfillment. Diversifying your income sources reduces risk, increases stability, and establishes a solid foundation for a profitable future.

Chapter 10: Key 4 - Asset Accumulation

Asset Accumulation as a Key to Financial Freedom
The emphasis in this chapter is on the critical role that asset accumulation plays in achieving financial freedom and living a prosperous life. The act of acquiring and expanding assets over time, which might include investments, real estate, enterprises, and other significant holdings, is known as asset accumulation. The primary idea is that by amassing assets, individuals can protect their financial future and, as a result, experience greater success and independence.

1. **Asset Accumulation**: Asset accumulation is a critical component of wealth creation. Individuals can increase their net worth by investing and saving sensibly over time. These riches give individuals a financial buffer, allowing them to follow their desires and goals.

2. **Financial Stability**: Putting together a diverse portfolio of assets can provide financial stability. Having assets can operate as a safety net in times of unforeseen expenses or economic downturns, preventing financial catastrophes.

3. **Passive Income**: A large number of assets create passive income. Real estate can generate rental income, stocks can offer dividends, and businesses can generate profits. These sources of income can help to minimize reliance on regular jobs and provide more financial flexibility.

4. **Retirement Planning**: Asset accumulation is critical for retirement planning. They can ensure a comfortable and financially stable retirement by

continuously increasing their wealth base.

5. **Entrepreneurship and Business**: Asset accumulation does not just refer to investments; it may also refer to the expansion of one's business assets. Growing a firm can result in higher earnings and wealth.

6. **Investment Methods**: The chapter may go into detail on various investment methods, such as stock market investments, real estate investments, and how to balance risk and reward in asset accumulation.

7. **Debt Management**: Debt management is an important part of wealth building. It is possible to investigate ways to reduce high-interest debt and leverage good debt for investments.

8. **Long-Term Perspective**: Successful wealth accumulation frequently necessitates a long-term outlook. The compounding effect can dramatically increase one's wealth over time.

9. **Diversification**: Spreading risk and increasing possible returns by diversifying assets

across multiple classes (e.g., stocks, bonds, real estate).

10. **Measuring Success**: The chapter may cover how to track and measure success in asset accumulation, as well as how to create particular targets and financial milestones.

11. **Mindset and Discipline**: Achieving financial freedom through asset accumulation necessitates discipline, a strong work ethic, and a deferred gratification mindset.

Asset accumulation is critical for generational wealth transfer for those interested in leaving a financial legacy for their heirs.

Finally, this chapter highlights that wealth accumulation is a planned and intentional process that can lead to financial freedom and, ultimately, a successful life. It gives people more control over their financial lives and allows them to follow their goals, interests, and aspirations.

Chapter 11: Key 5 - Tax Planning

Tax Planning as a Key to Financial Freedom for a Successful Life

In this chapter, we will look at tax planning and its importance in gaining financial freedom for a successful life. Tax planning is a purposeful and methodical strategy for controlling your tax liabilities so that your after-tax income and wealth growth are maximized. It is about making informed decisions to lawfully lower the amount of taxes you owe, not just filling out tax papers.

Here's a more detailed explanation of why tax planning is critical for financial freedom:

1. **Increasing Wealth Accumulation**: With proper tax preparation, you can keep more of your hard-earned money. By lowering your tax burden, you may invest and preserve a bigger amount of your income, which is

critical for long-term wealth accumulation.

2. **Legal Strategies**: Tax planning is not about evading taxes or engaging in criminal activities. It focuses on knowing and utilizing the tax system to your benefit. This includes taking advantage of all applicable tax deductions, credits, exemptions, and incentives.

3. **Long-Term Financial Objectives**: Tax planning is in line with your long-term financial objectives. It assists you in structuring your financial affairs in such a way that taxes are minimized not only this year but throughout your lifetime. This is especially crucial for retirement planning and asset transfer to heirs.

4. **Asset Protection**: Effective asset structuring can help shield your assets from undue taxation and prospective creditors. Trusts and estate planning, for example, can be utilized to protect your fortune for future generations.

5. **Investment Decisions**: The investments you make might have major tax consequences. Tax planning entails adjusting

your investment portfolio to reduce capital gains, dividend taxes, and other investment-related tax obligations.

6. **Business and Employment Considerations**: If you operate a business or work for yourself, tax preparation is even more important. Tax-efficient corporate structures can result in significant savings. Similarly, knowing the tax implications of employee benefits like stock options is critical.

7. **Changing Tax Laws**: Tax laws are always changing. Keeping up to date on these developments and changing your financial strategy as needed is an essential element of tax preparation. It can be costly to fail to react to changing tax regulations.

8. **Peace of Mind**: Effective Tax preparation brings peace of mind. It alleviates the stress of last-minute tax filing, lowers the danger of audits, and guarantees that you are taking full advantage of any available tax savings.

9. **Financial Independence**: The ultimate purpose of tax planning is to assist you in achieving

financial independence. You may achieve your financial goals faster if you keep more of your money and make it work for you, whether that's retiring early, starting a business, or pursuing your passions without financial restraints.

In conclusion, Chapter 11 emphasizes that tax planning is not an afterthought, but rather a critical component of financial success. It enables individuals and organizations to effectively, legally, and ethically navigate the difficult world of taxes, assisting them in securing their financial future and working toward their vision of a successful life.

Chapter 12: Key 6 - Retirement Planning

Retirement Planning as a Key to Financial Freedom for a Successful Life

Retirement planning is an important part of gaining financial freedom and living a successful life. In this chapter, we'll look at the fundamental components of retirement planning and why they're so important for your financial well-being.

1. **Understand Retirement Planning**: Retirement planning is the process of establishing financial goals and strategies to safeguard your financial security after you have stopped actively producing income. It entails saving, investing, and managing your finances to achieve a stress-free retirement.

2. **Financial Freedom**: Financial freedom entails having the resources and ability to live life on your terms, rather than being reliant on a steady paycheck. The cornerstone of gaining this freedom is proper retirement preparation. It enables you to maintain your standard of living and cover basic expenses even after you stop working.

3. **Longevity and Inflation**: Because people are living longer lives, retirement can span decades. Furthermore, inflation eats away at the purchasing power of your savings over time. Retirement planning ensures that your money lasts as long as you

do while also keeping up with escalating prices.

4. **Retirement Accounts**: Retirement accounts play a crucial role in achieving financial freedom and living a successful life. They offer tax benefits and serve as a means to save for retirement.

401(k): A 401(k) is an employer-sponsored retirement savings plan that allows employees to contribute a percentage of their pre-tax salary to a designated account. A percentage of these payments may be matched by employers. The funds grow tax-free until retirement when they are liable to income tax upon withdrawal.

Individual Retirement Account (IRA): An IRA is a personal retirement savings account that individuals can open and fund on their own. Traditional IRAs (contributions with pre-tax income, taxed upon withdrawal) and Roth IRAs (contributions with post-tax income, tax-free withdrawals in retirement) are the two types of IRAs. Both provide a variety of investment options to help you develop your retirement funds. By diligently contributing to accounts like 401(k)s, IRAs, and pension plans, individuals can secure their financial future, ensuring a comfortable retirement. This financial security allows for peace of mind, enabling one to focus on other aspects of a successful life, such as pursuing passions, traveling, or spending time with loved ones, without the worry of financial constraints.

5. **Investment Strategies**: As part of retirement planning, you must select appropriate investment strategies depending on your risk tolerance, timetable, and financial objectives. Diversifying your investments allows you to control risk while potentially growing your retirement funds.

6. **Social Security**: The chapter may discuss Social Security benefits and how they relate to retirement planning. Understanding how Social Security works is important if you want to maximize your retirement income.

7. **Healthcare and Long-Term Care**: Good retirement planning

should take into account healthcare costs as well as long-term care needs in retirement. Understanding Medicare, supplemental insurance, and preparing for unexpected medical bills are all part of this.

8. **Estate Planning**: Estate planning is an important element of retirement preparation. This includes drafting a will, establishing trusts, and naming beneficiaries to guarantee that your assets are transferred by your intentions.

9. **Debt Management**: Debt management and reduction are frequently addressed in retirement planning. In retirement, being debt-free or having a reasonable debt load can have a big impact on your financial security.

10. **Budgeting and Lifestyle Decisions**: The chapter may highlight the necessity of budgeting and making lifestyle decisions that are consistent with your retirement goals. To achieve financial freedom, it is critical to strike a balance between spending and saving.

11. **Seeking Professional Advice**: The chapter may emphasize the need to work with financial advisors or specialists to develop a personalized retirement plan that is tailored to your requirements and circumstances.

12. **Monitoring and Adjusting**: Retirement planning is a continuous process, not a one-time event. To stay on track, you must regularly analyze your investments and make adjustments to your strategy as needed.

Finally, Chapter 12 on retirement planning is critical for obtaining financial freedom and living a fulfilling life in your later years. You can take control of your financial future, protect your retirement, and enjoy the peace of mind that comes with knowing you've planned for the years ahead if you understand the principles and tactics presented in this chapter.

Chapter 13: Key 7 - Giving Back and Philanthropy

We will go into the fundamental concepts of giving back and charity as key aspects of gaining financial freedom, living a successful life, and contributing to the benefit of society in this chapter. This theme incorporates the belief that when combined with financial success, generosity may be a potent engine for personal fulfillment and societal improvement.

1. **Financial Freedom and Success**: Financial freedom is frequently defined as the ability to live one's desired lifestyle without relying on a single source of income. This chapter emphasizes that obtaining financial freedom is about more than just accumulating wealth; it is also about appreciating the value of giving back. Many successful people discover that embracing philanthropy as an intrinsic component of their financial journey propels them to new heights. Giving can be

extremely gratifying and provide a sense of accomplishment that exceeds financial success alone.

2. **Happiness Through Philanthropy**: Giving to charity causes has been shown to have a significant impact on one's sense of happiness and well-being. When people contribute to causes they care about, they gain a sense of purpose and happiness that transcends tangible prosperity. Knowing that your resources are making a difference in the lives of others might bring you a lot of joy.

3. **Improving Society at Large**: When individuals who have attained financial independence engage in philanthropic activities, they can have a societal ripple effect. Their contributions can be used to fund projects that address critical concerns such as poverty, healthcare, education, and environmental conservation. This, in turn, leads to the overall improvement of society. It can also motivate others to participate, resulting in a good circle of giving.

4. **Legacy and Long-Term Impact**: One of the chapter's primary themes is that true success lasts beyond one's lifetime. Individuals can leave a lasting legacy that will benefit future generations through generosity. Famous philanthropists such as Bill and Melinda Gates and Warren Buffett have illustrated this principle by pledging significant chunks of their money to charity causes, ensuring that their impact remains.

5. **A Holistic Approach to Achievement**: The chapter also underlines the need to view financial achievement and generosity as interconnected components of a holistic approach to success. Having financial freedom allows you to give back, and generosity boosts your entire sense of accomplishment.

In summary, Chapter 13 emphasizes the importance of giving back and philanthropy in gaining financial freedom and living a successful life. When people appreciate the importance of contributing to the well-being of others, they not only experience greater personal fulfillment and enjoyment, but they also play an important part in the advancement of society as a whole. This holistic approach to success recognizes that true prosperity is measured not just by personal money, but also by the beneficial impact one may have on the lives of others and the planet.

Part IV: Strategies for a Successful Life

Chapter 14: Mindset and Success

This chapter examines how having a growth mindset can be a strong technique for achieving success in a variety of areas of life. Here's an elaboration of the idea:

1. **Understanding Mindset**: The chapter begins by defining a mindset. It is a combination of beliefs and attitudes that influence how we see and

respond to our surroundings. The two basic mindset types described are the "fixed mindset" and the "growth mindset."

2. **Fixed Mindset**: A fixed mindset is defined by the assumption that our abilities and intelligence are permanent, immutable characteristics. People with a fixed attitude shun problems, give up quickly, consider effort as futile, disregard criticism, and feel frightened by others' achievements.

3. **Growth Mindset**: A growth mindset, on the other hand, is the concept that abilities and intelligence can be developed through hard work and perseverance. A growth mentality welcomes difficulties, perseveres in the face of setbacks, views effort as a path to mastery, learns from criticism, and finds inspiration in the success of others.

4. **Impact on Success**: The chapter underlines that the mindset one chooses has a tremendous impact on their potential for success. Individuals who have a growth mindset are

more likely to overcome barriers and achieve their objectives because they are willing to put in the work to improve and adapt.

5. **Resilience and Learning**: The growth mindset promotes resilience by encouraging people to see setbacks and failures as chances to learn and improve. People who have a growth mindset recognize that making mistakes is an inevitable part of the learning process.

6. **Effort and Achievement**: One important aspect to remember is that effort is not a sign of weakness, but rather a path to mastery. Effort is an important component of success, and those with a growth mentality are more likely to put in the time and effort required to thrive in their chosen industries.

7. **Real-Life Applications**: The chapter will most likely include examples and case studies of how adopting a growth mindset has led to success in many industries such as sports, business, and education.

8. **Practical Ways**: The chapter may also provide readers with practical ways for shifting from a

fixed to a development mindset. This may entail self-reflection, self-talk, goal planning, and seeking out difficulties.

In summary, Chapter 14 of "Mindset and Success" delves into the idea that mentality is critical in deciding one's road to success. Individuals are more likely to attain their goals and have successful lives if they adopt a growth mindset and view problems and efforts as chances for progress. This chapter is likely to provide practical guidance on cultivating and applying a growth mindset in numerous spheres of life.

Chapter 15: Time Management

"Time Management as a Strategy for Living a Successful Life," is an important issue for obtaining success in both personal and professional realms. The emphasis in this chapter is on how efficient time management may be a significant component in one's route to success. I'll expand on this idea for you.

1. **Recognize Time as a Limited Resource**: Time is a finite resource that can never be replaced. Successful people realize the value of time and how they allocate it has a significant impact on their success. This chapter emphasizes the significance of time management.

2. **Creating Goals and Priorities**: Time management begins with creating specific and attainable goals. Successful people do not work carelessly; they have a plan. They define their short- and long-term goals and prioritize them according to priority and timeframes.

3. **Time Management Planning**: Time management planning is critical for living a successful life. Setting clear goals, prioritizing chores, developing calendars, and breaking down goals into small parts are all part of it. This aids in time management, organization, and stress reduction. Regularly assessing and revising your plans helps you keep on track and

adapt to changing conditions, resulting in increased productivity and a more rewarding life.

4. **Removing Time Wasters**: Recognizing and removing activities that take time without adding to one's goals is an important part of time management. Excessive social media use, unneeded meetings, and ineffective multitasking are examples of this.

5. **Time Blocking**: Successful people frequently employ the time blocking strategy, in which they dedicate specified blocks of time to specific activities or categories of work. This aids concentration and ensures that important activities are accomplished.

6. **Delegation**: Another time management method is delegation. Successful people recognize that they cannot do everything themselves. Delegating duties to capable individuals or teams frees up their time for more vital obligations, resulting in more productive results.

7. **Adaptability**: Because life is unpredictable, this chapter may emphasize the value of flexibility. Successful people are versatile and can change their plans when unforeseen challenges or opportunities arise.

8. **Mindfulness and Work-Life Balance**: Success entails more than just fulfilling job objectives; it also entails striking a balance between work and personal life. It is critical to examine the importance of self-care and ensuring that one's personal life is not sacrificed for professional success.

9. **Continuous Improvement**: Time management is a continuous activity, not a one-time event. Successful people constantly assess their time management strategies and make changes as needed.

10. **The Cumulative influence of Effective Time Management**: In a successful life, effective time management can have a cumulative influence on financial freedom. You can boost your productivity and income over time by consistently committing time to actions that contribute to

your financial goals, such as work, investing, or study. As a result, you may save, invest, and develop wealth more efficiently. The cumulative effect of effective time management can lead to increased financial security and independence, ultimately contributing to a successful and affluent life.

Chapter 16: Networking and Building Relationships

When it comes to gaining influence for financial freedom and a successful life, networking and creating relationships are key components. This chapter emphasizes the importance of building a strong network and creating meaningful contacts to advance one's career and financial prospects. Here's a more detailed description of how networking and relationship-building can help you on your path to financial freedom and success:

1. **Access to Opportunities**: Networking provides access to a

plethora of opportunities. Connecting with a wide range of people exposes you to job options, investment opportunities, and company ideas that you might not have encountered otherwise. These opportunities can help you increase your income and generate wealth.

2. **Sharing of Information and Knowledge**: Developing ties within your sector or profession helps you to tap into a vital supply of information and knowledge. Your network can provide critical insights, market trends, and industry-specific updates for making sound financial decisions. Staying educated is an important component of financial success.

3. **Mentorship and Guidance**: Connecting with mentors and experienced individuals is an important part of effective networking. Their advice and mentoring can be quite beneficial in navigating your financial journey. Learning from the experiences and knowledge of successful people can help you get there faster.

4. **Joint partnerships**: Strong ties can lead to joint partnerships. Collaboration with like-minded people or business partners can result in collaborative investments, pooled resources, and creative company concepts. Collaborations can increase income sources and improve financial security.

5. **Increasing Credibility**: A strong network can attest to your competence and trustworthiness. It is simpler to recruit investors, clients, and business partners when you have a reputation for being dependable and professional. This credibility can help you succeed financially.

6. **Emotional Support**: Relationship building is about more than just business; it's also about emotional support. You will face obstacles and setbacks on your path to financial independence. Having a strong network might provide you with the emotional power to go through difficult circumstances.

7. **Resource Pooling**: Having access to a varied pool of resources, such as finance, skills, and relationships, is generally

associated with networking. This pooling of resources can assist you in a variety of financial undertakings, from launching a business to investing in real estate or the stock market.

8. **Personal Branding**: Effective networking can assist you in developing a strong personal brand. A good reputation in your sector or community can lead to increased demand for your services, higher fees, and better job chances, all of which can lead to financial success.

9. **Lifelong Learning**: Networking promotes lifelong learning and personal development. Staying current and improving your abilities might lead to promotions, raises in pay, or the potential to charge more prices for your services.

10. **Community Engagement**: Relationship building isn't just for professionals. Participating in your local community or social networks can also lead to opportunities, whether through donation, kindness, or building a good reputation.

In summary, Chapter 16 underscores the importance of

networking and connection building as a strategic approach to financial freedom and success. You can acquire access to opportunities, expertise, mentorship, and support by actively engaging with others, which can dramatically improve your financial chances and help you have a successful life. Not only what you know, but also who you know, can play an important role in your financial journey.

Chapter 17: Balancing Work and Life

We go into the essential topic of balancing work and life as a strategic approach to achieving financial freedom and a successful life in this chapter. The phrase "securing the bags" is frequently associated with financial achievement and wealth accumulation. True success, on the other hand, extends beyond monetary benefits and encompasses a fulfilling and well-rounded existence.

1. **Define Financial Freedom**: To begin, it is necessary to define financial freedom. This is the moment at which a person has amassed enough money and passive income to pay their expenses while also allowing them the opportunity to pursue their passions and interests without being bound to a 9-to-5 job.

2. **The Dangers of Overwork**: Many people feel that working long hours without rest is the way to financial success. However, this method frequently results in exhaustion, strained relationships, and a lower quality of life. It's critical to understand that working smarter, not simply harder, is a critical component of achieving financial independence.

3. **Work-Life Balance**: Achieving financial freedom necessitates a well-thought-out approach that balances work with other elements of life. This balance is essential for maintaining physical and mental health, nurturing relationships, and allowing for personal growth.

4. **Efficient Time Management**: The necessity of efficient time management is emphasized in this chapter. It advises readers to prioritize chores and delegate when needed to make time for personal activities and relaxation.

5. **Investing in Self-Development**: Financial independence is about more than just gaining money; it is also about personal development. The chapter recommends making time for self-improvement, whether by learning new skills, pursuing hobbies, or simply caring for one's well-being.

6. **Strong and Healthy Connections**: A successful life is built on strong and healthy connections. Balancing work and life allows people to spend more time with their loved ones, which can provide emotional support as well as opportunities for collaboration and networking.

7. **Avoiding Financial Pitfalls**: The chapter emphasizes the significance of avoiding typical financial pitfalls such as excessive debt or wasteful expenditure. Being financially responsible and saving for the

future are important aspects of balancing work and life.

8. **Setting and Reviewing Goals**: Individuals who set clear goals and often analyze their progress are more likely to achieve financial freedom and a successful life. This procedure ensures that one's efforts are directed toward the achievement of one's goals.

9. **Measuring Success Holistically**: The chapter finishes by underlining the need to measure success holistically. True success is measured not just by the size of your financial account, but also by your general well-being and pleasure.

In conclusion, Chapter 17 emphasizes the need to balance work and life as a strategic approach to obtaining financial freedom and a successful life. It questions the traditional notion of overworking for financial gain and highlights the value of holistic success, which includes not just wealth but also well-being, relationships, and personal development. Work-life balance is more than a plan; it is a way of life that can lead to a more satisfying and profitable future.

Part V: Putting It All Together

Chapter 18: Creating Your Financial Freedom Plan

1. **Establishing precise Financial Goals**: The chapter will most likely emphasize the necessity of establishing precise financial goals. Whether you're saving for retirement, purchasing a house, or establishing a business, setting financial objectives is the first step.

2. **Budgeting and Expense Management**: A crucial part of financial planning is budgeting. It entails keeping track of your income and expenses to ensure you're living within your means while still saving for your long-term goals. This chapter could provide specific budgeting strategies.

3. **Debt Management**: It is critical for financial independence to manage and reduce debt, particularly high-

interest debt such as credit cards. The chapter might go over ways to efficiently paying down debts and avoid further debt accumulation.

4. **Investment Strategies**: You will almost certainly need to invest to safeguard your financial future. Various investment choices, such as stocks, bonds, real estate, and mutual funds, may be discussed in this chapter. It may also address the significance of diversifying your investments to manage risk.

5. **Emergency Fund**: Creating an emergency fund is critical for dealing with unforeseen expenses without deviating from your financial strategy. The chapter may help you develop and maintain this financial safety net.

6. **Retirement Planning**: Planning for retirement is an important aspect of gaining financial independence. The chapter may go on retirement accounts such as 401(k)s and IRAs, as well as the need to make consistent contributions.

7. **Income Streams**: Having several income streams might provide additional financial

protection. This could include side jobs, investments, or other sources of passive income.

8. **Estate Planning**: Future planning also includes estate planning, which includes wills, trusts, and ensuring your assets are dispersed according to your intentions.

9. **Tax Strategies**: Managing your taxes effectively can have a big impact on your financial performance. Tax planning, deductions, and credits may be covered in this chapter.

10. **Consistent Review and Adjustments**: A financial plan should be evaluated and updated as your life circumstances change. The chapter may emphasize the significance of regular check-ins and plan adjustments.

11. **Financial Education**: It is critical to arm yourself with financial information.

12. **Mindset and Discipline**: Discipline and a good mindset are typically required for a successful financial plan. It could give you tips on how to stay motivated and devoted to your financial goals.

In conclusion, Chapter 18 on developing a financial freedom plan covers a comprehensive approach to financial success. Setting clear goals, managing costs, lowering debt, making strategic investments, planning for retirement, and maintaining financial discipline are all part of the process. To react to changing conditions and attain long-term financial stability in a dynamic environment, you must conduct regular reviews and revisions to your strategy.

Chapter 19: Sustaining Financial Freedom

Financial freedom is a multifaceted term that entails efficiently managing your resources to ensure a stable and prosperous future. Here's a detailed explanation of how to attain and retain financial freedom to live a successful life:

1. **Financial Planning**: Create a detailed financial plan that details your financial goals, budget, and investment methods.

Set specific, measurable, achievable, relevant, and time-bound. The goals should be S-M-A-R-T. This plan will be your success blueprint.

2. **Budgeting**: Budgeting helps you to track your income and expenses. Make sure that your spending does not surpass your income. Set aside a percentage of your salary for savings and investing. Your budget should be examined and updated regularly.

3. **Debt Management**: Repay high-interest debts such as credit cards and personal loans. Reduced debt allows you to save and invest more of your income. Avoid taking on unnecessary duties in the future.

4. **Create an emergency fund**: Create an emergency fund with at least 3-6 months' worth of living expenses. This fund will serve as a safety net in the event of unforeseen financial difficulties, such as medical emergencies or job loss.

5. **Investing**: Use your savings to make wise investments. Invest in a wide range of asset classes, including equities, bonds, real estate, and mutual funds.

Consider getting professional advice or conducting comprehensive research to make informed investment decisions.

6. **Financial Education**: Continue to learn about personal money. Keep up with financial news and trends. To improve your financial knowledge, attend workshops or seminars, study books, and investigate online resources.

7. **Passive Income**: Attempt to produce streams of passive income such as rental income, dividends, or royalties. These other sources of income can help to promote financial stability and lessen reliance on single employment.

8. **Contribute to Retirement Accounts**: Contribute to retirement accounts such as a 401(k) or an IRA to guarantee your financial future. The sooner you begin saving for retirement, the longer your investments have to grow.

9. **Living Within Your Means**: Avoid overspending on frivolous purchases. Make deliberate spending decisions and emphasize needs over wants.

This will allow you to save and invest more money that can be used for other relevant goals later.

10. **Tax Efficiency**: Consider the tax consequences of your financial decisions. Optimize your tax methods to reduce your tax liability, which can have a substantial impact on your wealth over time.

11. **Consistent Monitoring**: Review your financial strategy and portfolio frequently to ensure that you are on track to reach your objectives. Make changes as your financial circumstances and aspirations evolve.

12. **Risk Management**: Have insurance coverage in place to protect yourself and your assets from unforeseeable catastrophes such as accidents, illness, or natural disasters.

13. **Generosity**: Include philanthropy and charitable giving in your financial plan. It can be enjoyable and add to your overall sense of accomplishment and purpose.

14. **Contribute to retirement accounts**: Achieving and maintaining financial

independence can be challenging. Prioritize your mental and emotional well-being since they are critical to living a successful and satisfying life.

15. **Flexibility and Adaptability**: Be adaptable and flexible in the face of changing circumstances. Because life is unpredictable, your financial plan may need to be adjusted.

To summarize, achieving financial freedom is a lifelong path that requires careful planning, disciplined financial habits, and ongoing education. It's not only about collecting wealth; it's about putting your resources to use to live a successful and fulfilled life while having the financial security to weather life's hardships.

Conclusion

In "Secure The Bag: 7 Keys To Financial Freedom and Investing Wisely For A Successful Life" by Richmond Sterling, readers embark on a transformative journey towards financial empowerment. This comprehensive guide not only provides invaluable insights into building a solid financial foundation and making wise investments but also lays out a roadmap to achieve true financial freedom. With a focus on key principles such as income generation, debt management, and philanthropy, this book equips readers with the tools to secure their financial future. Through the integration of strategies for a successful life, including mindset, time management, and networking, Sterling underscores the holistic approach to financial well-being. In the end, readers are empowered to create their own Financial Freedom Plan, setting them on a path to lasting prosperity and fulfillment. This book is a must-read for anyone seeking to secure their financial future and lead a successful life.

Recommendation

I highly recommend "Secure The Bag: 7 Keys To Financial Freedom and Investing Wisely For A Successful Life" by Richmond Sterling. This comprehensive 5-in-1 book covers everything from building a strong financial foundation to strategies for a successful life. It's a valuable resource for anyone looking to improve their financial literacy and secure their financial future. The book provides practical advice and actionable steps to achieve financial freedom and invest wisely. Don't miss out on this insightful guide to managing your finances and building a successful life.

Review Enquiry

Dear readers,
I would greatly appreciate your valuable insights and feedback on my book, "Secure The Bag: 7 Keys To Financial Freedom and

Investing Wisely For A Successful Life" by Richmond Sterling. Your input will play a crucial role in shaping future editions to better serve your financial goals and needs.

Please share your thoughts on how this book has been of help to you.

Your feedback will help me ensure that "Secure The Bag" continues to be a valuable resource for achieving financial freedom and success.

Below is my author page URL for your valued feedback and reviews.

https://www.amazon.com/author/richmondsterling

Thank you for your time and support!

Sincerely,

Richmond Sterling